Seeing Both Sides

# School Dances, Yes or No

Erin Palmer

Rourke
Educational Media

rourkeeducationalmedia.com

*Scan for Related Titles and Teacher Resources*

## Before Reading:

### Building Academic Vocabulary and Background Knowledge

Before reading a book, it is important to tap into what your child or students already know about the topic. This will help them develop their vocabulary, increase their reading comprehension, and make connections across the curriculum.

1. *Look at the cover of the book. What will this book be about?*
2. *What do you already know about the topic?*
3. *Let's study the Table of Contents. What will you learn about in the book's chapters?*
4. *What would you like to learn about this topic? Do you think you might learn about it from this book? Why or why not?*
5. *Use a reading journal to write about your knowledge of this topic. Record what you already know about the topic and what you hope to learn about the topic.*
6. *Read the book.*
7. *In your reading journal, record what you learned about the topic and your response to the book.*
8. *After reading the book complete the activities below.*

### Content Area Vocabulary
*Read the list. What do these words mean?*

acknowledge
alleviate
development
element
grooming
inclusive
navigate
occasion
predicament
scrutiny
socializing

## After Reading:

### Comprehension and Extension Activity

After reading the book, work on the following questions with your child or students in order to check their level of reading comprehension and content mastery.

1. *What is an opinion? (Summarize)*
2. *How do personal experiences shape someone's opinion? (Infer)*
3. *Why would a school want to host a dance for students? (Asking questions)*
4. *Have you been to a school dance? What was it like? (Text to self connection)*
5. *What other activities could schools host for students to socialize with each other? (Asking questions)*

### Extension Activity

Take a poll of your classmates' opinions about school dances. Create a chart showing their responses.

# Table of Contents

# Taking Sides

School dances can be fun and enjoyable for some but awkward and stressful for others. It depends who you ask. A room full of people at the same event can have entirely different experiences.

If you and a friend go see a movie together and afterward, someone asks how the movie was. You answer "Awesome!" Your friend says "Awful!" You both saw the same movie, but you each have a different opinion about it.

Your opinions are based on personal preferences, how much information you have on the topic, and your past experiences. Sometimes your own opinions can change over time as you learn more and have new experiences.

School dances are something many people feel differently about. Let's consider arguments from both sides.

Reality ✓

Students start learning the skills needed to form an opinion from a young age. The reasoning and critical thinking skills needed to form an opinion are taught as early as kindergarten.

# School Dances? Yes, Please!

School dances can be the perfect opportunity to have a few hours to spend time not thinking of assignments, upcoming tests, or pending projects. Instead, you can have fun with friends, relieve some stress, and learn to deal with new emotions in a safe place.

Students have to deal with a lot of pressure. Classes can be difficult. In addition to the academic pressure, there is also a lot of social pressure. It can be hard to make time for your friends when you are so busy with classwork all of the time.

School dances give you something fun to look forward to. Planning and decorating can help you make new friends and be creative with a theme for your dance.

The social **element** of school dances is very important. Students don't always get to spend much time **socializing** in class.

Though technology has opened up new ways to communicate through texting, emailing, and gaming, it has also made it harder to connect in-person. School dances let students have fun together without a screen between them.

Reality ✓

Children spend an average of seven hours per day using some sort of media for entertainment.

Aside from being a fun way to enjoy spending time with your friends, school dances can also help you develop social skills that are important for developing healthy relationships as you get older.

It can be confusing when you experience new feelings. First crushes are a natural part of growing up, but learning how to deal with them can be really tricky.

School dances can help you **navigate** through these new feelings in a supervised location without being pressured. Talking or dancing can let you interact with your crush in a fun and age-appropriate way.

School dances can help you improve your social and emotional learning. These skills are just as important to learn as academic subjects, especially when you are young.

Reality ✓

The importance of social and emotional learning has been proven by many studies.

Research shows that dancing is also helpful for social **development**. Dance can also help you connect with your body in a way that boosts self-esteem and helps you feel more confident.

Dancing in a supervised setting actually teaches students how to **acknowledge** and respect the personal space of others.

## Reality ✓

Dance can help with social and emotional learning and physical and cognitive development.

It is also important for students to have somewhere safe to spend time with one another. School dances are usually held in a location like a gym or auditorium.

Students may stray off path and spend time in places that aren't safe or with people who aren't trustworthy. School dances are full of students you already know and take place under the watchful eyes of teachers and parents.

Even when students are trying to behave, it can be hard to control the peer pressures that can come up when you are not in the right setting. Some may want to leave and go somewhere else, which could put you in quite a **predicament**.

Reality ✓

Peer pressure can be both spoken and unspoken, according to the U.S. Department of Health and Human Services.

School dances **alleviate** that element. Students are typically not allowed to leave unless they are picked up by a parent, and strangers are not allowed in, so you don't have to worry about meeting someone who might be dangerous.

Going to a school dance is so much more than dancing and getting dressed up. You don't even have to dance if you don't want to. It is all about the experience.

Attending a dance is a fun way to make memories with your friends, talk to students in different classes or other grades, and develop crucial social skills.

School dances are a part of growing up. They are fun but they are also full of important social lessons.

# School Dances? No Way!

Despite what movies and TV programs show, school dances are not often perfect evenings.

It costs the school money to host a dance. Sure, ticket sales cover some of those costs, but when you factor in food, drinks, music, decorations, and other costs, dances can get expensive.

**Reality ✓**

Schools have to do a lot of fundraising to host events like school dances. But many parents are frustrated with the large amount of fundraisers that schools require.

Even if it doesn't cost much to organize a dance, it is still money that could go toward something that benefits the entire student body.

With so many budget cuts in schools, is it right to waste money on something like a dance? There are plenty of things schools actually need that are more educationally important.

Education Fund

Reality ✓
Most states are providing less funding per student than they were during the recession of 2007-2009, according to experts.

Even with chaperones, students might bring in things they are not supposed to or behave in ways they shouldn't.

Dancing might seem fun, but it can also get out of control. No one wants to be put in a situation where an innocent dance ends up making you feel uncomfortable. The chaperones can't be everywhere at once, so in the darkened room, it can be easy for some students to take dancing too far.

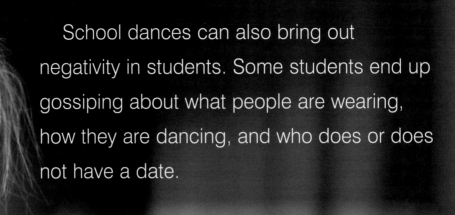

School dances can also bring out negativity in students. Some students end up gossiping about what people are wearing, how they are dancing, and who does or does not have a date.

**Reality** ✓

About 34 percent of students have been bullied at school, according to the National Center for Education Statistics.

It can be stressful for students who are trying to enjoy themselves to have to face **scrutiny** and whispers from some of their classmates. With bullying already such a major issue at so many schools, dances can bring out some of the worst behavior in students.

Students will want to look nice for such a special **occasion** so they may want to buy a new outfit or spend money on **grooming**.

For students who don't have a lot of money, dances can be stressful. If they want to go but can't afford to buy a ticket, it can be disappointing. If they manage to get a ticket but can't afford the clothes or other costs that come with prepping for a dance, it can be embarrassing.

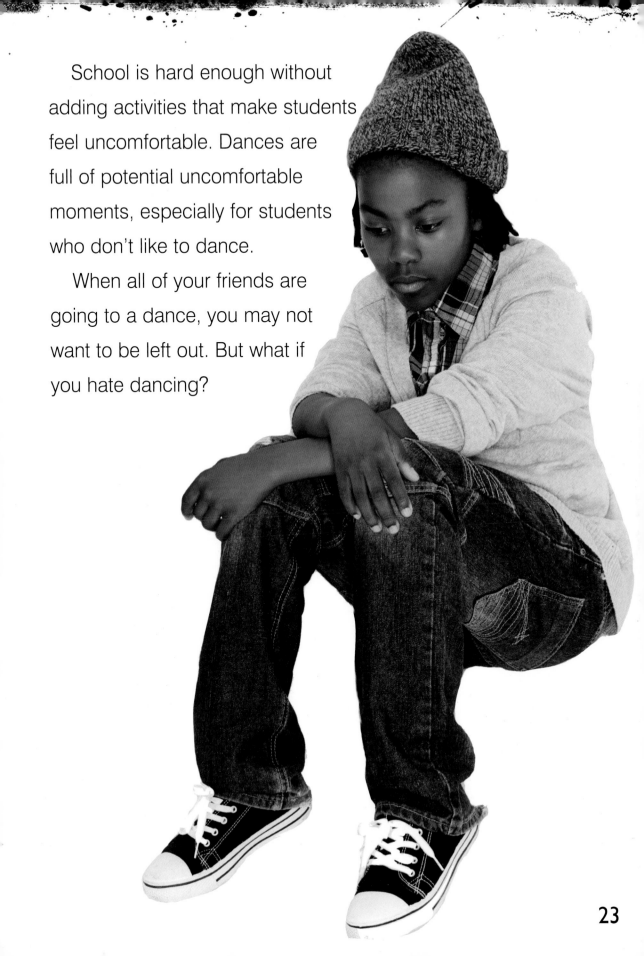

School is hard enough without adding activities that make students feel uncomfortable. Dances are full of potential uncomfortable moments, especially for students who don't like to dance.

When all of your friends are going to a dance, you may not want to be left out. But what if you hate dancing?

If you go to a dance just to spend time with your friends and they all hit the dance floor, you may be left in an uncomfortable position. Do you give in and go dance even though you really don't want to? Or do you stay behind all alone?

If you do want to dance and no one asks you, it is an awful feeling. Why go somewhere that might make you feel bad about yourself when you are supposed to be having a good time?

Either way, it can make you feel uncomfortable. And dances are supposed to be fun, right?

What many school dance organizers forget is that creating a fun event is not a one-size-fits-all effort. In other words, dances can be boring. Movies, television shows, and other forms of pop culture prove dances have pretty much been the same old thing for decades.

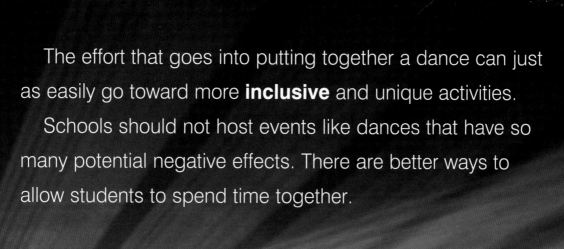

The effort that goes into putting together a dance can just as easily go toward more **inclusive** and unique activities.

Schools should not host events like dances that have so many potential negative effects. There are better ways to allow students to spend time together.

# Your Turn

Now that you have considered school dances from different points of view, are you in favor of them or not? Why do you feel that way? Even if you agree with points from both sides, you can use the specific examples and information to decide

which side you feel more strongly about.

Once you know which side of the argument you fall on, you are ready to write about your own opinion. Use what you learned in the book, but add your own personal experiences and information to make your argument stronger.

Your point of view is important, and so is learning how to express it!

# Telling Your Side: Writing Opinion Pieces

- Tell your opinion first. Use phrases such as:
  - *I like* _____.
  - *I think* _____.
  - _____ *is the best* _____.
- Give multiple reasons to support your opinion. Use facts and relevant information instead of stating your feelings.
- Use the words *and*, *because*, and *also* to connect your opinion to your reasons.
- Clarify or explain your facts by using the phrases *for example* or *such as*.
- Compare your opinion to a different opinion. Then point out reasons that your opinion is better. You can use phrases such as:
- *Some people think* _____, *but I disagree because* _____.
- _____ *is better than* _____ *because* _____.
- Give examples of positive outcomes if the reader agrees with your opinion. For example, you can use the phrase, *If* _____ *then* _____.
- Use a personal story about your own experiences with your topic. For example, if you are writing about your opinion on after-school sports, you can write about your own experiences with after-school sports activities.
- Finish your opinion piece with a strong conclusion that highlights your strongest arguments. Restate your opinion so your reader remembers how you feel.

# Glossary

**acknowledge** (ak-NOL-ij): to admit to be real or true

**alleviate** (uh-LEE-vee-eyt): to make easier to endure; lessen

**development** (dih-VEL-uhp-muhnt): the act or process of developing; growth

**element** (EL-uh-muhnt): a part of a whole

**grooming** (GROO-ming): to tend carefully as to person and dress; make neat or tidy

**inclusive** (in-KLOO-siv): including a great deal, or encompassing everything concerned

**navigate** (NAV-i-GATE): to find one's way

**occasion** (uh-KEY-zhuhn): a special or important time, event, ceremony or celebration

**predicament** (pri-DIK-uh-muhnt): an unpleasantly difficult, perplexing, or dangerous situation

**scrutiny** (SKROOT-uh-nee): close and continuous watching or guarding

**socializing** (soh-shuh-lahy-zing): to associate or mingle sociably with others

# Index

# Show What You Know

1. How can your personal experiences make for a stronger argument in an opinion essay?

2. Why should you use research to help make your point?

3. Could reading or listening to a strong argument get you to change your position? Why or why not?

4. What do you think is the most important part of making a strong argument and why?

5. Why is it important to be able to see both sides of an issue?

# Websites to Visit

http://aieconversation.org/conversations/social-emotional-learning-and-arts-education

www.timeforkids.com/homework-helper/a-plus-papers

www.classroom.synonym.com/fun-ideas-shy-people-first-dance-15657.html

# About the Author

Erin Palmer is a writer and editor in Tampa, Florida, who lives with her three dogs: Bacon, Maybe, and Lucky. She enjoyed school dances, but wished they would have played a better variety of music. Erin loves to go on trips and spend time on the beach.

**Meet The Author!**
www.meetREMauthors.com

Edited by: Keli Sipperley

Cover design and Interior design by: Rhea Magaro

**Library of Congress PCN Data**

School Dances, Yes or No / Erin Palmer
(Seeing Both Sides)
ISBN 978-1-68191-384-1 (hard cover)
ISBN 978-1-68191-426-8 (soft cover)
ISBN 978-1-68191-466-4 (e-Book)
Library of Congress Control Number: 2015951551

**Also Available as:**

Printed in the United States of America, North Mankato, Minnesota